Can Birds Get Lost?

Illustrations by
John Rice, Tom Powers, and Mimi Powers
Cover illustration by Tom Powers

Text copyright © 1991 by Highlights for Children
Illustrations copyright © 1991 by Boyds Mills Press
All rights reserved
Published by Bell Books
Boyds Mills Press, Inc.
A Highlights Company
815 Church Street
Honesdale, Pennsylvania 18431
Printed in Mexico

Publisher Cataloging-in-Publication Data
Myers, Jack, 7/10/13
  Can birds get lost? : and other questions about animals / answered by
Highlights science editor Jack Myers.
[64]p. : col. ill. ; cm.
Includes index.
Summary : Dr. Jack Myers answers questions posed by children about animals.
Many questions taken from columns in *Highlights for Children.*
ISBN 1-878093-32-0 HC ; ISBN 1-56397-401-0 PB
1. Animals—Juvenile literature. [1. Animals.] I. Series. II. Title.
591—dc20   1991
Library of Congress Catalog Card Number 90-85911

1 0 9 8 7 6 5

Can Birds Get Lost?

And Other Questions About Animals

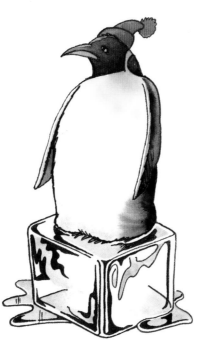

Answered by

Highlights Science Editor
Jack Myers, Ph.D.

BOYDS MILLS PRESS

Welcome Aboard!

You have joined our club. We are the curious, wondering about all the interesting things that happen in our world. When we don't know, we ask. Here in the records of our club you will find answers to some of the questions you have wondered about.

For the past thirty years readers of Highlights for Children have been asking me questions. And I have been helping them find answers. There have been questions I could not answer and questions that I think no one could answer. Science has always been like that, and it is like that today even in the world's greatest laboratories. It is our ignorance—what we don't know—that drives us to learn more. That's what science is all about.

I have been fortunate in having as friends many scientists who have helped me find answers. To all of them we are grateful, for they have broadened our understanding.

In this book some of the answers have been written directly by people who had a much greater understanding of the questions than I. Some were written by Dr. Clark Hubbs and by the late Dr. Osmond P. Breland. Each of their answers will be acknowledged by their initials.

Jack Myers

Jack Myers, Ph.D.

Is the platypus a mammal?

Carla Della Vedova
Brightwaters, New York

The platypus usually is considered to be a mammal because its features are like those of other mammals. For example, it has hair over most of its body and has mammary glands that make milk for its young. It also has pretty good temperature control so it can be called warm-blooded.

One characteristic, however, that is more like the reptiles is that the female lays eggs which develop outside her body.

A platypus is a water-loving animal that lives along streams in Australia. You probably have heard about it because it is partly like a reptile and partly like a mammal.

Actually, it should be no surprise that there are some animals that do not fit exactly into groups like reptiles and mammals. After all, these names just stand for man-made ideas.

I am quite sure that a platypus doesn't care whether we think it's a mammal or a reptile.

Why do fish live in pet stores but not at home? They die about two days after I get them. Why?

Robin Mirsky
Hicksville, New York

I doubt that I can tell you why. The trouble is that there are a number of possible reasons. I think the first thing to do is to go to the pet store and ask for advice. But I can tell you some of the problems you need to solve in order to keep fish as pets.

One problem with fish is to keep enough oxygen in their water. You and I get our oxygen from the air around us. Fish get oxygen from the water. Water does not hold much oxygen. So there must always be some way to keep putting oxygen into water, usually from air, to replace what the fish are using up. Cool water holds more oxygen than warm water. So usually it is best to keep fish in a cool place.

Another problem can arise from chlorine in our water. Usually it is added to our water to kill bacteria. Chlorine is not very good for fish. One way to get rid of the chlorine is to let a bowl of water stand open for a day.

Another kind of problem occurs with fish if you feed them too much. Most fish really do not need much food. Overfed fish are not likely to be healthy.

Some fish are easier to keep than others. Goldfish have been used as pets for years and years partly because they are easy to keep.

I have tried to tell you some ideas about fish that may be helpful. But my best advice is: Ask someone who already has fish and knows about how to keep them.

Do fish sleep?

Yvonne Blanchard
Kilgore, Texas

Yes, I would say that fish do sleep. Some fish actually lie on the bottom at night. Some of them even produce a gooey covering as a protection against other fish who might be looking for an easy meal. In the dark many fish have a lower rate of metabolism (their body machinery slows down), and that is much like sleep.

But there is one thing you do in your sleep that fish do not do. You close your eyes. Fish can't do that. They don't have any eyelids.

How come the goldfish in my aquarium swallow the gravel and then spit it out?

Debbie Farrall
Grand Island, Nebraska

I can think of two reasons why you might see your fish mouthing gravel. Goldfish eat a wide variety of food, especially the very tiny plants (algae) and animals that grow on the surface of pebbles and rocks. One way for a goldfish to get this goody is to pick up a pebble, scrape off the algae in its mouth, and then spit out the pebble.

There is another possible reason. Most fishes have very special routines or rituals that they use in courtship. One of these is nipping at the surface of things about them. If a fish were nipping at the gravel bottom of an aquarium, it would seem to be picking up pebbles and spitting them out again. So a male goldfish behaving this way might not be eating at all but only trying to impress a female goldfish nearby—or vice versa.

C.H.

Since male deer shed their horns, how come you rarely find the horns in the woods?

Annie Reeves
Jeddo, Michigan

I have wondered about that, too. I decided to ask a young friend, Scott Wendlandt, who has spent a lot of time watching and studying deer. Here is what he told me:

First, you must consider that deer range over rather wide areas, maybe twenty acres or more. Just to find a set of antlers within twenty acres, even when the antlers are first shed, would take careful searching and some luck. A second reason is that such rodents as squirrels and rats like to chew on antlers, perhaps because of the calcium or phosphate that they contain.

Scott says that he has found only about twenty cast-off antlers, even after years of looking for them. And most of those were partly chewed up. It's interesting to realize that even deer horns are recycled in nature.

Why do rabbits jump instead of just running away?

Denise Saucier
Uxbridge, Massachusetts

You are right that rabbits have a special way of moving around. They go in jumps or hops one after the other.

Rabbits have long and strong back legs. They take off on a hop with a big push from their back legs. They land on their front legs and then bring the back legs forward to get ready for another hop.

If you were built like a rabbit, I think you might travel that way, too.

8

About two days ago a deer was by my house. He was so tame you could pet him. The conservation department told us he was only eight months old. Much construction is taking away the homes of wildlife. Can you tell me if I can help?

*Kelly Rozewicz
Cheektowaga, New York*

Kelly, I understand and worry about that, too. The places where your home is and where my home is were once part of wild America. There are more and more people on this earth, and we take up more and more space. That leaves less and less for other animals. But we really shouldn't get mad at people who build new houses just because our houses were built first.

I don't know any way to solve the problem except to do everything we can to set aside areas for wildlife. Some animals learn to live with people better than others do. Raccoons and deer seem able to get along pretty well. Of course, deer don't get along well in the cities. But in spite of all the new construction, there are many more deer in New York State now than there were one hundred years ago.

I think we all need to understand the problem and then do whatever we can.

I would like to know why ants can carry so much when there are very few people who can carry even one hundred pounds?

Kelly Jones
Denver, Colorado

It is true that most insects, including ants, are comparatively stronger than people. By using a special kind of machine, it has been found that the average insect can pull about twenty times its weight. On this same kind of machine, a man cannot even pull his own weight.

An ant can lift more than fifty times its weight with its teeth, and a beetle has lifted several hundred times its weight on its back. If a man could do as well, he could lift almost four tons with his teeth, and carry more than sixty tons on his back. If a man could jump as well as a flea, compared to size, he could jump the length of several football fields, and more than four hundred feet high. A man would not want to jump this far or this high. He would splatter all over the ground when he landed.

There are several reasons that insects are so strong. One is their small size. A small animal is comparatively stronger than a large animal. If an insect were as large as a man, it would not be nearly so strong compared to its size. Another reason insects are so strong is the way insect muscles work differently and better than the muscles of people.

How do ants walk on the ceiling without falling off?

Kevin Clough
Oak Forest, Illinois

I haven't been able to find an answer in any books, so I asked my friend, Larry Gilbert, who is an entomologist studying insects. He is not sure, but he thinks that many insects have tiny bristles or short hairs on the bottoms of their feet. If that's true, the hairs must be tiny—small enough to hold on to very small irregularities in the surface.

Some insects, maybe ants, can walk on the underside of glass. Of course, even glass has a rough surface when seen by a powerful microscope.

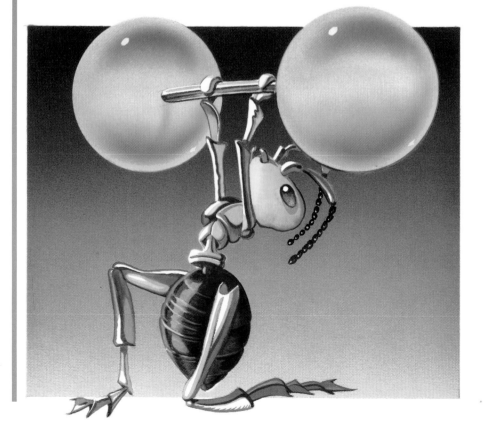

I have tons of mosquito bites. They are driving me crazy. Why do mosquito bites itch?

Laura Monick
North Tonawanda, New York

When a female mosquito sticks her beak into your skin to get a meal of blood, she leaves a little of her saliva in the wound. I guess almost all humans are allergic to something in mosquito saliva. So, we get an allergic reaction, and the skin around the bite itches and gets red.

Why do ladybugs (or ladybirds) have dots? We have a collection of them and have been looking in books and encyclopedias for the answer. We hope you know.

Judith and Donna Stasmey
Normal, Illinois

If you have been making a collection of ladybugs, I think you must know more about them than I do. (I had to do some looking up in books, too.)

I think you already know that ladybugs are small beetles, that they belong to the family of insects called the Coccinellidae, and that they are helpful to farmers because their larvae eat aphids.

It seems that ladybird beetles (as they are also called) live all over the world. And there are supposed to be about 350 different kinds or species in the United States.

I don't even know whether all kinds of ladybird beetles have spots, and I would not be sure that it was a ladybird if it did not.

I have a cat named Puff. One day she was sitting in my bedroom window. I could see Puff's reflection in the glass. Could she see her reflection?

Carrie Lancaster
Wagoner, Oklahoma

I think the answer is yes. Animals can see their reflections just as you and I can. Your cat, Puff, must even know that the reflection she sees is her own and is not another cat.

A cardinal that lives in my yard is not so smart. Often he comes to my bedroom window very early in the morning and wakes me up by pecking against the window. He seems to be fighting his reflection as if it were another cardinal moving into his territory.

Why do cats always arch their backs and hiss when they are alarmed?

Mary McGuire
Penns Neck, New Jersey

I didn't know the answer to your question, so I asked Lory Frame for help. Lory, who is a naturalist, has written many articles about animals. Here is what she had to say:

When a cat arches its back and hisses, it feels it is facing a dangerous enemy. In most cases the cat is not eager to fight. It would rather just escape. So it pulls itself up to look big and frightening enough to make the enemy think twice. That's when the cat gets the chance to run away.

As for hissing, that's a threat, too. Mother cats defend their babies by hissing at intruders, and sometimes they even hiss at their own kittens. This sends them scurrying

back to the nest. The hiss is so alarming that the kittens learn to be more cautious when that particular enemy appears again.

Many animals hiss as a way of scaring each other. I have seen vultures in Africa threaten each other during squabbles over food by spreading their wings and hissing. This makes them appear bigger and more frightening. And once, when I was little and visiting my grandmother, a big white goose of hers hissed at me when I peeked inside the coop to look at her nest full of eggs. Did I ever jump!

When animals are frightened or want an enemy to back off, they may try to appear more dangerous than they really feel. But there is something we should remember: If a frightened animal is cornered or pushed too far, it will use whatever weapons it has to defend itself. In the case of cats, the weapons are sharp teeth and claws. Many dogs and people have discovered that.

My dog M.J. had five puppies. I think she mated with five dogs. Do you know why? She had a white pup with black spots, two brown pups, a black one with white spots, and a brown one with white spots.

P.S. Their names are Marble, Penny, Spots, Pacific, and Mercury.

Paula Scheerer
Pasadena, Maryland

Different-color puppies are not really so unusual. I think that all of them may well be full brothers and sisters. Differences in color are only differences in pigment in the skin, "only skin deep," and not really very important. You can easily see differences among human brothers and sisters in hair color, eye color, and just how they look. In fact, that's common in most animals.

You may be thinking of dogs that have been "pure bred," such as collies. Collies look like collies because they've been "selected" for hundreds of years. If collies are always mated to collies, then their puppies look like collies and have almost the same coloration.

But if dogs are not purebred, then their puppies may have the same variations that we see in many wild animals.

I hope you still like your puppies.

I have a dog that whines when I play the harmonica. Is she crying or singing?

Stacy Hickey
Poughkeepsie, New York

I did not know the answer to your question, so I sent it to our friend Dr. John J. Mettler. Dr. Mettler is a veterinarian. Here is what Dr. Mettler said about your question:

It is not uncommon for dogs to try to imitate sounds they hear. For instance, some dogs howl when they hear a fire siren, and a boy I knew had a dog that used to sing when the boy played the violin. If a dog hears a sound it doesn't like, it will run and hide, so I expect the dog is singing.

Why don't birds get shocked when they sit on wires?

Sajan Eapen
Houston, Texas

That does look surprising. Birds sometimes sit on wires carrying thousands of volts and held up high by big towers.

Living things, like birds and people, can get shocked by touching two different wires or touching one wire and the ground. Then electricity has a way in and out, and can flow through a body and give a dangerous shock.

For example, you will notice that the cord to an electric lamp or an electric motor always has at least two wires to carry electricity in and out.

A bird on an electric wire is safe and happy—unless it makes the mistake of touching another wire at the same time. Then it's a dead bird.

How come owls have very big eyes?

Sharona Shotkin
Patchogue, New York

The eyes of owls are different from those of most birds. They are large, and both eyes are located on the front side of the head.

If you watch birds, you will notice that most of them have their eyes located on the sides of their heads. They can look at something with one eye at a time. This helps them look for food on the ground. And it makes it easier for the bird to see a cat that might be sneaking up on one side.

Because its eyes are in front, an owl cannot see to one side without turning its head. But it can use both eyes together, the way you do, to help judge distance to whatever it is looking at.

How do birds lose their feathers and then grow back their feathers so they are not bald?

Debra Suerstonas
Thomaston, Connecticut

Feathers are remarkable gadgets. I am sure that if anyone could find a way to build anything as strong and yet as light, they would wish to patent the process.

Feathers are made from a hardened protein, called keratin, about the same kind of stuff that you use to make hair and fingernails.

The feathers you see on a bird do not contain any living cells. But each one is made by a collection of cells in a little pocket or follicle in the skin. A bird has several different kinds of feathers and each follicle can produce only one kind. The follicles are lined up on the

skin to make a pattern which is special for each kind of bird.

Since feathers contain no living cells, they cannot be repaired when they get broken or worn. So most birds have a regular schedule of replacing feathers once or twice a year. In molting, an old feather slips out of its attachment and a follicle starts building a new feather. Most birds replace their long flight feathers only a few at a time, which seems a sensible way to go about it.

I guess the answer to your question is that birds do not get bald because their follicles keep working to make new feathers.

We humans have hair instead of feathers. Hair is nice. Losing it and being bald is an inconvenience (as I know very well). But for a bird, being bald would be a catastrophe. I am sure you can see why.

When a bird flies, why don't its wings get tired?

Rayna Polsky
New Britain, Pennsylvania

No one really knows whether a bird gets tired flying. I suspect that sometimes they do.

Birds that are in the air most of the time—or those that fly long distances in migration—fly rather slowly. A muscle that works steadily and slowly can be made to work without getting tired. (Think about your heart muscle.)

Some birds, especially larger ones, spend a lot of time soaring on air currents. They don't need to flap their wings when they soar. You have noticed that many birds do not fly all the time. Most of them, such as the ones around my bird feeder, seem to do a lot of resting.

Was Brontosaurus really afraid of Allosaurus? Was Triceratops afraid of anything?

Scott Carlson
Elk Grove, Illinois

Everything we can say about dinosaurs comes from studying fossil remains. Teeth tell about what the animal ate. The shape and size of bones tell about the animal's size and strength. And tracks preserved in the rock tell about how an animal walked. By comparing fossil teeth and bones with those of other animals, we get ideas about how an animal looked.

Brontosaurus is pictured as a very large, blimplike, plant-eating animal. Just from its jaws and teeth we know that Allosaurus must have been a meat-eater. No one will ever know what a Brontosaurus thought about. Its skull had room for only a very small brain, so it could not have done much thinking.

However, I can say that if I had been a Brontosaurus I surely would have been afraid of that vicious-looking Allosaurus.

Triceratops got its name from its three sharp horns. These stuck out of a big bony shield that protected it in front. Sometimes it is compared to today's rhinoceros. If I had been a Triceratops, I think I wouldn't have been afraid, except maybe of a bigger Triceratops.

If a paleontologist finds a fossil, he will know how long ago it came from. How does he know?

Jordy Moldofsky
Toronto, Ontario

I asked my friend Jack Wilson to answer your question. He is a paleontologist. Here is what he said:

Telling particular kinds of animals apart is no different than telling different makes of automobiles apart.

A paleontologist is a person who has studied fossil animals enough so that he can tell the bones of one animal from another. Like the differences between cars, there are differences that he looks for to help him identify bones.

Telling the age during which an animal lived is like trying to learn the year a car was made without the auto company records. The paleontologist has three clues. First, all fossils are found in rocks, and those rocks and fossils that are on the bottom are oldest. By fitting together stacks of rock and fossils from various places, he works out ages in terms of older-than or younger-than.

Secondly, animals, like cars, have changed with time. Generally the older ones are simpler and the newer ones are more complex. The third clue sometimes is available if the fossil bones are found with certain minerals which are radioactive. These minerals can be analyzed in a way that tells how old they are.

I was wondering if dinosaurs had trunks like elephants. At the Melbourne Museum there was an exhibition of dinosaur fossils. Near the Mamenchisaurus was a skeleton of an adult elephant, and there were no bones where the trunk would be. How do scientists know that the dinosaurs in the flesh had no trunks?

Sunil Daniel
Bendigo, Australia

I see what you mean. Fossils are made from the bones of an animal's skeleton, not from the muscles and soft parts of its body.

If you look again at an elephant skeleton in the museum, you should notice the large nasal bones about the mouth. If these have been preserved on the skeleton, you will see that they are just right for attaching a trunk.

Something that is as big and heavy as an elephant's trunk needs a good strong bone for its attachment to the skull.

A human skull or a dinosaur skull has a nasal bone that is enough to support a nose sticking out in front, but not a long trunk. So you can tell from the fossils that humans and dinosaurs never had trunks.

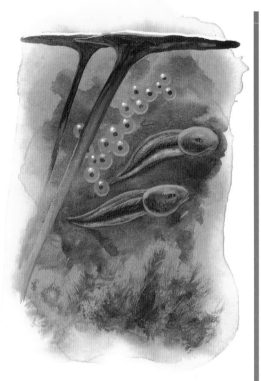

Can frogs breathe underwater?

Jonathan Phipps
Tatla Lake, British Columbia

The answer is yes, but I need to say something more.

A frog has two ways of breathing. It can breathe air into its lungs much as you do. It also can do some of its breathing through its skin. That means it can get some oxygen from the water around it and get rid of carbon dioxide, too.

When you scare a frog sitting at the edge of a pond, it takes a big gulp of air as it dives in. The frog is not very active underwater and doesn't need to breathe very fast. So, once the big gulp of air is used up, the frog continues to breathe through its skin. That works all right if the water is cool, but it doesn't work so well if the water is warm. Warm water doesn't hold as much oxygen. And warm water speeds up the frog's metabolism so it needs more oxygen. Soon it will come out for a real breath of air.

I want to know what tadpoles eat. I've got tadpoles in an aquarium, and they always stay in the gravel you use when you have fish. Why?

Billy Saylor
Mokena, Illinois

I think that tadpoles feed mostly on algae and other plants growing in the water and maybe also on small pieces of dead animal material. As you must have noticed, they can swim, but they often spend a lot of time resting and attached to something. Maybe that is why they stay mostly in the gravel.

I hope you were successful in raising some of your tadpoles and able to watch them change into little frogs.

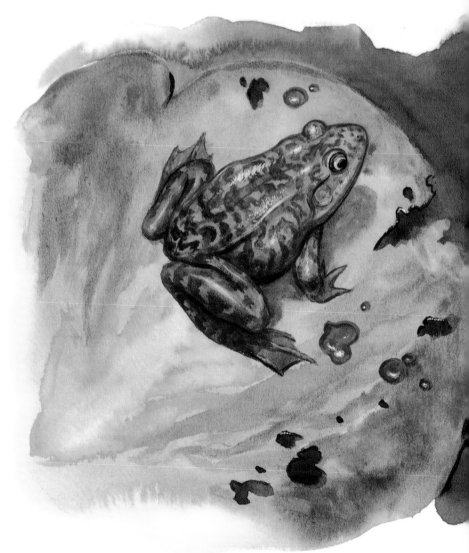

My friend has a toad. I asked my dad if you could get warts from it, but he didn't know. Is it true?

Angie Lucey
Janesville, Wisconsin

I know that some toads are warty-looking animals. But I think they are safe. I can't find that anyone ever got warts from a toad. So I think you can even try petting your friend's toad, if it looks cuddly enough.

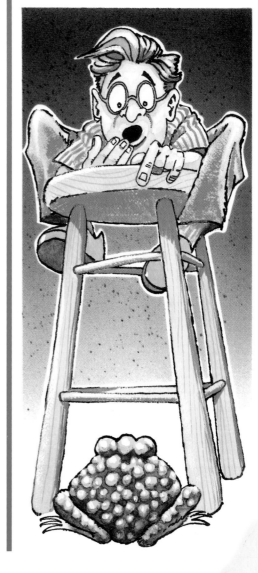

What is the difference between a frog and a toad?

David Dion
Framingham, Massachusetts

Toads and frogs are amphibians and need to live in water at least during part of their lives. But toads are able to spend much of their lives on dry land, while most frogs stay closer to water.

Toads differ from frogs in other ways, too. Toads usually have shorter hind legs and are not as good at hopping, and their skins are often dry and warty-looking.

Are killer whales really mean?

Ashley Katen
Glenrock, Wyoming

Killer whales are sometimes called the "wolves of the sea."

They are predators—they need to eat other animals to make a living. And, like wolves, they work together in groups.

If you're a porpoise or a big fish, I suppose a killer whale looks pretty mean because it wants to eat you. If you're a killer whale, then you hope that the porpoise or big fish doesn't get away—because then you would have to go hungry.

After you've thought about this you can decide on an answer to your question.

Do piranhas and sharks really eat people, or do they just bite and then swim away?

Soo Mie Kwon
Belleview, Missouri

Sharks and piranhas do not feed on people very often, but both have been known to eat people. They go about this in different ways.

Of the many kinds of sharks in the ocean, a few are considered dangerous because of attacks on people. A large shark could easily eat a person and a few have been known to do this. When a shark attacks a person or an animal, it often swims by rapidly and takes a bite as it passes. After eating the bite, the shark usually returns. Sometimes sharks may go away after biting a few times, but the person or animal is usually severely injured, especially if the shark is a large one. Sometimes more than one shark will attack an animal or person.

Piranhas are much smaller than sharks, and they live in some of the rivers in South America. There are several kinds of piranhas that are several inches to a foot or so in length. A single piranha is much too small to eat a person.

However, hundreds of these little fish travel together in groups or schools. When a school of piranhas attacks a person or other animal, each fish takes a bite as it swims by. Then each fish comes back for more.

If the school is a large one, this may continue until only the animal's skeleton remains. A large school of piranhas is not at all likely to just bite and then go away.

O.P.B.

Do whales really spit water?

Megan Wolf
Fairport, New York

I think you are asking about the whale spouts or water spouts that whales make when they come to the surface. If you are, then the answer is no.

Most kinds of whales have their nostrils (like your nose) on top of their heads. When they come to the surface after a dive they want to get some fresh air. (As you probably know, they are air breathers like you and me and not gill breathers like fishes.)

Before whales can take in a breath of fresh air, they need to breathe out the old air from their lungs. They do this in a big whoosh. All that warm air has lots of water vapor that condenses out as water droplets and may also carry a little sea water along. That makes a water "spout" that may be seen for miles so that whale watchers can say, "Thar she blows."

I would like to know why dogs pant when they are not tired.

Colin McClelland
Buena Vista, Colorado

The answer is that dogs sometimes pant just to help cool off.

When your body temperature gets too high, you sweat. Evaporation of water takes up a lot of heat. Evaporation of sweat from your skin helps cool your body when its temperature begins to get too high.

Dogs (and cats, too) are pretty well covered with hair and have very little bare skin. They can't keep cool by sweating—except maybe a little from the pads of their feet. Instead, a dog pants. That moves air rapidly back and forth over the moist tissues of its mouth and tongue.

Panting is the dog's way of evaporating extra water to help keep its body cool.

I have had two dogs in my life and have seen lots, too. But the thing I'm lost about is: How do they bark?

Carrie O'Donnell
Ariss, Ontario

I guess I really do not know either. I can only tell you something about it. If you watch a dog, you will see that its ribs and chest get smaller very quickly to make the bark. That means that it is driving air out of its lungs and up through its windpipe and mouth. That's also what you do if you suddenly shout, "Hey."

I think a dog's bark is like your shout. What I do not know is why a bark sounds like a bark. I suppose the special sound, just like one of yours, is made by a dog's vocal cords.

My cat can see in the dark. How?

Stacy Peterson
Two Rivers, Wisconsin

In really and truly complete darkness no animal can see. Our eyes and those of other animals see only by light rays that come to them. However, there are not many places in nature where there is complete darkness with no light rays at all. Even on a dark night there is a little light from the stars that gets through clouds.

Our eyes are good at seeing with just a little light. Some animals that hunt at night are much better. Cats and owls can see when there is so little light that you would say it was completely dark. I think that's what people mean when they say that a cat can see in the dark.

Is a dog's tail a voluntary or involuntary muscle? This has been puzzling me for a long time.

Elaine Stensbol
La Habra, California

A dog's tail must be moved by a voluntary muscle. As you know, a voluntary muscle is one you can control from the brain. An involuntary muscle is one which you cannot control by thinking about it—like the muscle in your heart.

I see why you might ask the question. A dog wags his tail as if that were an automatic response when he is pleased. There are many kinds of animal (and human) behavior like that. You can pretty well count on a person smiling or laughing if he is pleased, or crying if he is hurt or very sad. The muscles that do those things are voluntary muscles, but they often work together in some special pattern.

Each kind of animal has its own special patterns of behavior. Tail wagging is a special pattern of dog behavior.

23

I read in many stories that elephants are afraid of mice. Is it true?

Donna Delattre
Ayer, Massachusetts

At one time many people thought elephants were afraid of mice. It was believed the reason for this fear was that the mouse might get into the end of the elephant's trunk. The idea was that the mouse might scratch the lining of the trunk or plug up the trunk so the elephant could not breathe.

It is now known that none of these beliefs are true. In zoos, mice have been seen running about very near the tip of an elephant's trunk, and the elephant did not pay any attention to them.

Elephants have a very keen sense of smell, and they depend on this to warn them of danger. They may not be able to see mice on the floor, but they certainly can smell them as the mice scamper about near the tips of their trunks.

The hole at the end of an elephant's trunk would be a strange hole for a mouse. I do not believe a mouse would run into this strange hole without looking in first. By the time the mouse could have looked into the end of the trunk, the elephant would have smelled it. The elephant could then "snort" and blow out a little air which should keep the mouse out of the trunk.

It may be that a mouse has gotten into an elephant's trunk at one time or another. If so, I have never heard or read of it. In fact, I cannot imagine why a mouse would want to get into an elephant's trunk!

O.P.B.

How do snakes hear?

Kristi Wilson
Memphis, Tennessee

Snakes do not have ears outside the head as we do, nor do they have ear openings or eardrums. We have parts of our hearing apparatus, called the inner ear, inside the head, and snakes have these parts also.

When a person or animal walks, it makes vibrations which pass through the earth to the body of the snake. It has been known for a long time that snakes can feel vibrations from the ground. The vibrations pass through the skin and muscles of the snake to a bone connected to its inner ear. From this bone, the vibrations pass to the inner ear, which "hears" them.

It is now known that snakes can also hear noises or vibrations that travel through the air. The vibrations caused by noises are also called sound waves. When people and most animals hear, sound waves strike the eardrum and go to the inner ear, which is sensitive to the sound waves or vibrations. Snakes do not have eardrums, but their skins, muscles, and bones carry the sound waves to the inner ears. In this way snakes can hear sound carried by the air, but probably not so well as we can.

What is it that makes some snakes poisonous?

Ashlee Gray
Marietta, Georgia

Some snakes are venomous. They have little needlelike fangs that inject a milky fluid when the snakes bite. The fluid is called a venom because it contains poisons. Since I didn't know what the poisons are, I had to do some reading. I was surprised to discover that there are whole books written about snake venoms.

There are different kinds of venomous snakes. Their venoms are not all alike, but they have some common features. Almost all of their chemicals are special proteins, not just one but a number of different kinds. Some are neurotoxins, which poison nerve endings so that they cannot carry nerve messages. Some make blood clot and plug up veins so that blood cannot flow. Some cause a breakdown of the membranes around red blood cells so that the cells break up and no longer work in carrying oxygen. Some of them are enzymes that dissolve some of the gluelike stuff that holds cells together.

Snake venom helps a snake digest its food. Think of a rattlesnake that has just struck a mouse and injected some venom. The snake can't do any chewing and swallows the whole mouse. Digesting big lumps of food is a slow job. That's why you chew your food before swallowing. If the rattlesnake injects some venom into the mouse before it dies, that is a way to get enzymes all through the body of the mouse. Then the whole mouse—not just its surface—is easy for the snake to digest.

After reading about rattlesnake venom, I think I will carefully stay away from rattlesnakes.

Are horses vegetarians?

Jill Landis
St. Louis, Missouri

I asked Dr. John J. Mettler, a veterinarian, to answer your question. Here is his answer:

Yes, horses are vegetarians. When talking about animals we usually use a different word that has almost the same meaning. We could say they are herbivores. Like cows, deer, goats, sheep, and rabbits, horses eat only plants. There is another group of animals that, in nature, live on meat. Dogs, wolves, and cats such as lions, tigers, and house cats are called carnivores. Pet dogs have learned from their owners to eat foods other than meat, but for a healthy diet they do need some meat.

There are some animals, called omnivores, that eat both meat and plants. These include bears, pigs, raccoons, and humans.

You can make a good guess about whether an animal is a carnivore or herbivore by noticing how its eyes are placed. A herbivore usually has eyes on the sides of its head. That helps it see all around to watch for danger. A carnivore usually has eyes that look straight ahead. That's a good arrangement for an animal that must chase its food.

My friend says her horse is hyperactive. Can horses really be hyperactive?

Renee Hoppens
Friendswood, Texas

I think a clue to the answer to that question is: People are not all alike. Some are nervous and excitable and like to be always moving. I guess that's what you mean by hyperactive. I think some horses are, too. Some of them are said to be jittery or frisky or high-strung. I think that means about the same thing.

It is easy to see that people are not all alike, and horses are also not all alike in their behavior.

Why are baby goats called kids?

Eileen Milliken
Drexel Hill, Pennsylvania

I don't know and I doubt that we will find out. The first meaning of "kid" given in my dictionary is "baby goat." And it seems that almost that same spelling is also used in other languages. So that word and meaning must have been used for a long time.

Another, and later, meaning of "kid" is a young person—like you. I don't know how that meaning got started. Maybe because, like young goats, young people are playful animals. Does that sound OK?

Do chickens have ankles?

Alex Padilla
Cincinnati, Ohio

Your question puzzled me. I do not really know much about chickens, so I asked my friend Kathy Dodge to answer your question. Kathy lives on a small farm near us and sometimes does illustrations for HIGHLIGHTS. She has two pigs, fifteen sheep, two cows, and a large flock of chickens. Here is her answer:

I hoped my chickens could show me where their ankles were, but they couldn't. I looked in some books instead. I found out that the legs of birds are almost the same as the legs of other animals, but the part that you might think of as the ankle is called the shank (or tarsus). This is the straight thin part between the foot, claws, or toes, and the joint near the body. The rest of the bird's leg is hidden under the bird's feathers. These are the leg and the thigh, the parts you eat if you have chicken legs for supper.

So I guess we could say chickens do have ankles, but we usually only talk about the feet, shanks, legs, and thighs.

Richard Bedard
Waterbury, Connecticut

A turtle has a very strong heartbeat. As a matter of fact, college students often use a turtle in studying the heart and its beat.

A turtle, like other reptiles, actually has a heart built a little differently from yours. A turtle's heart has three chambers whereas yours has four. But in having a heart that keeps thumping away to pump blood, a turtle's heart works very much like yours.

How do turtles get their shells?

Andrea Lynn
Horsefly, British Columbia

The shell is part of the turtle's body, and the young turtle has the shell when it hatches from the egg. The shell develops or grows in the egg just as do other parts of the body. It grows around the turtle's body and becomes connected to the ribs and to the backbone.

The part of the shell on the back is called the carapace, and the part under the tummy is the plastron. The carapace and the plastron are connected together on each side by a bony plate. Some people believe that a turtle can crawl from its shell, but this is not true. It has no more chance of crawling from its shell than it has of going off and leaving some other part of the body.

Since a turtle has a shell, parts of its body are different from other animals. One of these differences is in the parts of the skeleton called the shoulder blades. Your shoulder blades are the flat bones on the back just behind where the arms are attached to the body. In people and other animals, the shoulder blades are outside the ribs. In turtles, the shoulder blades are inside the ribs.

Another difference is where the front legs attach to the skeleton. In turtles, this attachment is inside the ribs. In other animals the attachment is outside the ribs.

I guess it is no surprise that a turtle has to have a special arrangement of some of its bones to fit them inside its shell.

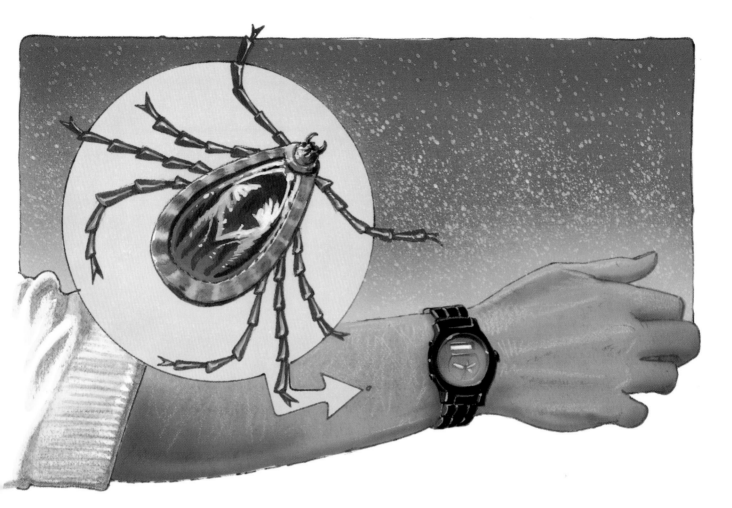

Wood ticks bother me very much. What are they good for?

Dawn Thatcher
Superior, Wisconsin

When most people ask that kind of question I think they really mean to ask, "What good are wood ticks to me as a human?" That is a question we might ask about other living things. What good is a mosquito? What good is a rattlesnake? To us as humans there are many organisms that seem to be a nuisance—or are really dangerous. And I do not know any simple way to answer that kind of question.

Many living organisms have developed and live together in the world. Each of them plays its own special role in nature. A biologist would say that each one fills an ecological niche.

As humans we are only one of the kinds of animals in nature. Because we are so smart, we have become the dominant kind of animal in the world. Maybe because we are so powerful, we are also likely to be arrogant. That leads us to think the rest of nature ought to be arranged just for us. And that leads us to look at some living things and ask what good they are to us.

We might turn your question around and ask: "Do I have a greater right than a wood tick to live on earth?" Or we might wonder: "If a wood tick could think, how would it ask the question?" It might ask: "What good are humans to me?"

I believe we should think of ourselves as a part of nature rather than that nature is made just for us. If you are willing to think of wood ticks as a part of nature, then you have answered your question.

Is the inky liquid an octopus squirts out poisonous?

Jessica Richardson
Hopkinton, Massachusetts

When alarmed, the octopus squirts out that cloud of inky liquid behind it. The cloud is like a smoke screen to cover its escape. The brown or black cloud is inky because it contains a lot of a common animal pigment, melanin. In fact, the original sepia ink comes from the ink sacs of cuttlefish, which are close relatives of the octopus.

The ink may also contain some chemicals which poison the smell receptors and help discourage a predator. But I think the smoke screen effect is more important.

We went to an aquarium and saw many fish. We also saw an electric eel. How does an electric eel make electricity?

Barbara Kurcz
Niles, Illinois

I don't know all about electric eels but I can tell you a little about them. The first idea is that all animals (and plants, too) make some electricity. Tiny electric currents flow in a nerve fiber when it is carrying a message and in a muscle cell when it is working.

Some fishes like the electric eel specialize in making electricity. They have special muscle cells called electro-plaques. These work like tiny batteries. Thousands of them are lined up lengthwise along the fish and can be discharged all at once to give a discharge of up to a thousand volts. I understand that the fish use this as a way to kill or scare away their enemies.

There are also other electric fish that can't give a big shock but can create a small electric field around them. Then they can detect anything that gets close and changes that electric field. So they have an "electric sense."

I guess the main idea is that electricity is something common in all animals on a very small scale. Some animals have become specialized to use electricity on a large scale.

Does a goldfish have any means of defense?

Lisa Koeller
Naperville, Illinois

I am not an expert on fish, but I can't think of any special means of defense that a goldfish can have. Goldfish are really special varieties of carp which have been bred in captivity for thousands of years. But even wild carp do not seem to have any special means of defense against being eaten by bigger fish.

When you said "means of defense," I suppose you were thinking about some way in which an animal can fight back if attacked. There are many animals which cannot fight back. Some of them can run or swim fast to escape, some of them hide, some of them just try to stay out of the way of possible attackers.

I have watched minnows in a lake near where I live. They have no means of defense against a hungry bass. But the bass never find all of them and there are minnows living in that lake year after year.

Do fish drink any kind of liquid?

Kelly Mitchell
Carson, California

I don't see how a big fish could swallow a minnow or a worm without getting some water, too. So I expect that any fish must drink at least some of the water around it.

Of course, it is no surprise if a freshwater fish drinks the water around him. You and I drink the same water, usually from some river or lake where fish live.

What about fish that live in the salt water of the ocean? You and I cannot drink much ocean water. It contains too much salt and would make us sick. But a saltwater fish can. In fact, he has to drink some to stay alive. Saltwater fish have a very special way of getting rid of salt through their gills.

Most freshwater fish, such as goldfish or black bass, cannot live in the ocean. They do not have that special way of getting rid of salt. So, like you and I, they can't drink salt water.

31

While studying my science, I read that cold-blooded animals must hibernate to survive cold. Why is it that bears, which are mammals and warm-blooded, need to hibernate?

Angela Sun
La Palma, California

There are many animals, even insects, that become dormant or inactive and hide away during the winter. I guess most people would say that such animals are hibernating.

Some zoologists, the scientists who study animals, have become very fussy about what should be called hibernation. The idea is that true hibernation is something special. It occurs only in warm-blooded animals, in fact, I think only in bats and in rodents such as the woodchucks and ground squirrels.

In hibernation the animal seems to be almost dead. Besides being asleep, it has a much-lowered body temperature, a lowered heart rate, and a lowered breathing rate. And it is so asleep that it warms up and wakes up very slowly. For true hibernation an animal's body machinery must be turned down until it is just barely alive, and then its machinery must be turned up again to wake it up.

It was a surprise to me to discover that bears do not have true hibernation. Of course, they hole up in a den for a winter sleep. But they may wake up many times during the winter. And they wake up more easily than true hibernators do. In fact, if you should find a sleeping bear during the winter, it is not a good idea to kick it.

Cold-blooded animals do not hibernate, simply because they have no control of their body temperature at all. Getting cold just turns them off until they warm up again in the spring. So what about a frog that spends the winter burrowed in the mud of a pond? I guess you should say that it is dormant.

Now that I have said all this, I should also say that not everyone uses the word hibernation in the same way. I have decided that it is best not to correct anyone or to get into arguments about it. Just understanding what people mean usually is good enough. That's what language is for.

Why do animals have fur?

Suzanne Spoelhof
Jenison, Michigan

Every animal needs a protective layer on its outside. Some animals like beetles and crabs and turtles have hard shell layers on their outsides. Most other animals have a protective layer of skin.

For most of the warm-blooded animals skin is not enough to help them keep warm. Birds have feathers and mammals have hair. Some mammals have hairs that are tightly packed and cover most of their bodies. I guess you would call that fur. That helps keep them warm.

Humans don't have much hair, except usually on top of the head. So we wear clothes. Maybe that's better than fur all over our bodies. It's easy to put on more clothes to stay warm or to take off some clothes to stay cool.

I would like to know the reason that animals can stand cold weather better than a person can.

Cindy Pepin
North Sterling, Connecticut

Of course there are many animals which cannot stand cold as well as a human. Most of the animals living in the tropics would never make it through a snowy winter, even if they could find enough to eat.

I suppose you are thinking about arctic animals like the polar bear and walrus. Their bodies are built for living in the cold. On the outside they have a thick fur or a layer of fat which helps to hold their heat inside. I suspect that their body machinery is arranged better to help conserve their body heat. And many of the arctic animals have special habits of living which help, too.

There are few places in North America where humans could live all winter without any clothes or houses to keep warm. Our skin is thin and not much of a cover. But we have learned how to protect ourselves and live in hot deserts, on the polar ice caps, on the floor of the ocean, and even out in space.

Can you think of any other animal which can live in so many different kinds of places as the human? It is very unlikely that any other animal ever stepped on the surface of the moon before a human named Neil Armstrong.

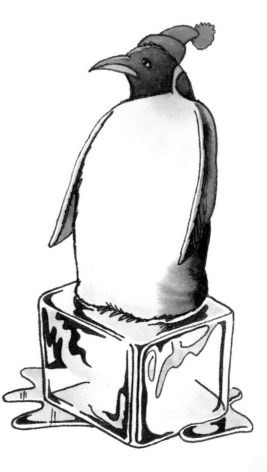

Where were dinosaurs first discovered and how did they get their name?

Christine Albaugh
Weston, Michigan

There is a reason that your questions are hard to answer: When dinosaur fossils were first discovered no one knew what they were. And it took some time to get used to this idea that there were animals long ago which became extinct without ever being seen by people.

One account I have read tells about fossil jaws that were discovered in a chalk quarry in Holland about 1770. They were first thought to be the jaws of a gigantic lizard. Later an Englishman by the name of Conybeare gave the animal (whatever it was) the name Mosasaurus. Once people began looking, a number of other fossil animals were found.

In 1841 Richard Owen decided that this whole group of animals, mostly very large, almost but not quite like lizards, ought to have a name. He called them the dinosaurs.

That's the best story I can find to answer your question.

I would like to know how many dinosaurs there were in the old days.

Stuart Pelle
Mapleton, Illinois

There is no way to get a very certain answer to your question. The dinosaurs lived during a long period of geologic time that lasted more than one hundred million years. That period is called the Mesozoic. Geologists usually say that the Mesozoic period ended about sixty-five million years ago. So you see, dinosaurs lived on earth during a long period of the earth's history. And not all the different kinds lived at the same time.

I found a partial answer in a recent article. A scientist who studies dinosaurs thought about the question. He counted all the different kinds of fossil dinosaurs that have been discovered: 285 kinds in the last 150 years. Recently scientists have been digging up about six new kinds every year. But you can see that our rate of making new discoveries will slow down as we get closer to finding all of them. So he estimated that there must have been about 1,000 different kinds.

If you want to be a dinosaur hunter, it's good to know that there are still hundreds of kinds waiting to be discovered.

When scientists find dinosaur bones, how do they know what bones belong to which dinosaur?

Kim Shively
Dayton, Ohio

I have never worked on fossils, but I have a friend and neighbor who does. Sometimes my children (when they were younger) would find a skull or some bones and ask me what kind of animal they came from. Usually I did not know, but my friend could tell them right away.

When they asked him how he could tell, he would answer them something like this: Suppose you found an old fender or bumper or windshield of a car. If you took it to a mechanic, he could tell you just what make of car it belonged to. Figuring out what bones belong to what kind of animal is something like figuring out that some particular shape of a fender belongs to some particular make of car.

Of course, figuring out how to fit fossil bones of dinosaurs together is tougher because no person ever saw a live dinosaur. But if you study enough dinosaur bones, you can figure out which ones must have fitted together.

I just got some rabbits. How long do rabbits live if they're in a cage? And how many days shouldn't you touch a newborn rabbit?

Justin Taylor
Sioux City, Iowa

The best place to find precise answers to your questions is from a pet store owner or a handbook on rabbit care. Your librarian will help you locate the handbook. Ideally, however, you should return to wherever you bought your rabbit and ask the store owner or pet breeder to share his knowledge with you.

Although I can't give you exact answers, I can tell you that a caged rabbit will enjoy a longer life if it's given good care, frequent attention, and even brief "vacations" in a fenced yard during warmer months. Be sure to supplement the animal's diet with fresh grass and other greens.

A good rule of thumb to follow regarding newborn bunnies is to leave them in the care of their mother until they begin to hop around on their own and leave the nest. At that point they're ready for all the love you can give them.

My hamster's eyes turn blue at night. He doesn't act sick, but his eyes are usually black. Do you think there's anything wrong with him?

Sara Blackwell
San Anselmo, California

I suppose that your hamster always looks OK the next morning. If that is true then his blue eye color at night must have some other explanation.

I have never looked into a hamster's eyes in dim light as at night. I expect that its eyes will seem to glow a little like those of other animals. The glow is called eyeshine. It comes from light reflected by a reflecting layer at the back of the eye. And it usually is colored a little by the reflecting layer.

At night a cat's eyes seem greenish, a raccoon's eyes are yellow. Maybe you have discovered that a hamster's eyeshine is blue. Do you think this might be the explanation?

How and why do cats purr?

Robert Dubel
Phoenix, Arizona

That is a question often asked and hard to answer. Below is one answer I have seen:

"The cat's hyoid apparatus, which helps hold up the voice box and support the tongue, is shaped like a capital U. This lies around the top of the windpipe and voice box. The closed end of the U goes up in back to touch the skull behind the cat's ear. It is made up of a chain of little bones. This chain holds the voice box and the tongue up close under the base of the cat's skull. There is not much room for movement up and down. The house cat and some other wild relatives have this hyoid apparatus. They purr, while other cat-family members do not have this arrangement and cannot purr. It is believed that the hyoid apparatus is what generates purring."

However, I must tell you that I once asked my zoologist friend, Dr. O.P. Breland, about this and he was not sure. So I am not sure, either.

You also asked *why* cats purr. I don't know an answer to that question.

If you find an answer, please let me know.

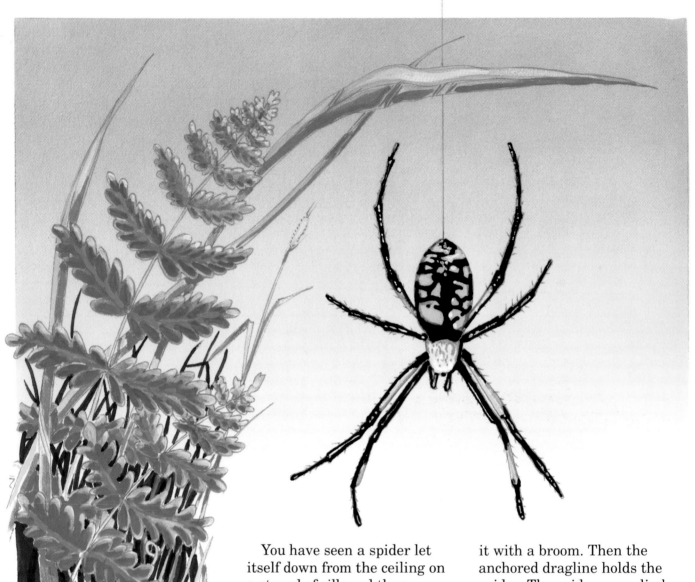

I have a puzzling question: A spider is hanging on his web from the ceiling. If you touch him, he will go up. But what happens to his web? Does he gather it up as he goes back to the ceiling, or what happens to it?

Nancy Stearns
Oakland, Oregon

You have seen a spider let itself down from the ceiling on a strand of silk and then scramble back up again. As it climbs, it catches the strand on one of its legs and rolls the silk into a ball. When the spider reaches a safe place, it will drop the ball of silk, or may even eat the silk if it is hungry.

A single strand of silk by which a spider suspends itself is called a dragline. As the spider wanders about, it pays out the dragline behind, and every once in a while attaches the line to the surface.

Sometimes the spider will deliberately jump off into space, or it may jump because an irate house cleaner punches it with a broom. Then the anchored dragline holds the spider. The spider may climb back to its former perch, or it may lower itself farther until it gets to another surface.

Spider silk, of which there are several kinds, is secreted from glands within the spider's body. The silk comes out through one or several finger-like structures called spinnerets located on the under surface of the body and toward the rear end. The silk comes from the body as a liquid but quickly hardens.

Spider silk for its size is among the strongest materials known. It is stronger than a steel wire of the same size.

I would like to know the meaning of the firefly's glow.

Salvatore Mangano
Flushing, New York

Maybe you already know that many living things can make light by a chemical reaction in their bodies. Light made this way is called bioluminescence. We know a lot about the special chemical reaction. But we do not know all about how it makes light.

In the firefly all the bioluminescence occurs at the end of the abdomen, so it might be called a tail light. The firefly can turn that light on and off to make a signal. In the evening the flashing lights you may see from fireflies come mostly from flying males. The females are more likely to be resting. When a female sees a flash from a male close by, she responds with a flash of her own.

Fireflies use their glow as the special means of signaling between males and females.

Can you tell me what fireflies eat and how to make a zoo with them?

Cheng-Jil Chen
Bayside, New York

Fireflies are not flies at all,

but they are kinds of beetles. They are also called lightning bugs. Firefly eggs hatch into little wormlike creatures called larvae. Some kinds of larvae glow in the dark, and those that do are called glow-worms. The glowworms eat very small creatures such as other insects, snails, and slugs. Some adult fireflies also eat other insects. Some eat pollen and other flower parts, and some probably do not eat anything at all.

It would be very hard to make a firefly zoo because, so far as I know, no one has been able to raise fireflies in captivity. But it is fun to capture several of them and watch them make their lights. The light of each firefly blinks on and off, but if there are several in a jar, some of their lights will be flashing most of the time.

I am very interested in chameleons. I would like to know how chameleons change their color, and also when they shed their skin.

Dwayne Walker
Newport News, Virginia

A chameleon is a special kind of lizard. It has big eyes and a long tongue with which it catches insects to eat. It also has a tail that can hold on to branches, and it has a body of different shape than other lizards. As you know, a chameleon can change the color of its body.

There are no true chameleons in the United States. But there are some lizards that can change the color of their bodies. For this reason these lizards are called the American chameleons. They are also called anoles.

These lizards can change color from green to brown or from brown to green.

Chameleons and other lizards can change colors because of some color cells they have in their skins. The color is changed because these color cells change size and shape.

We do not know everything that causes lizards to change color. One thing that helps is what the lizard sees. Other things are how the lizard feels and whether it is hot or cold. Neither chameleons nor any other lizards are always the same color as the stuff they are sitting on.

The American chameleon feeds on insects. As it grows, it sheds its skin from time to time. If it gets lots of food it sheds its skin more often.

Anoles or American chameleons are found where there are many vines, plants, and flowers. They can find lots of insects to eat in places like this, and they sometimes climb bushes and trees.

O.P.B.

I have a newt. My parents say not to touch him too much because his skin may be poisonous. Is this really true?

Claudia Dupont
Edmonton, Alberta

It is true that some frogs and salamanders have some stuff in their skins that is poisonous—at least poisonous enough to make a dog sick if it ate one. I am sure you are not planning to eat your newt and I doubt that there is any danger in touching it.

However, you should also think about your newt and how it will be happiest. It needs to keep its skin moist and probably does not like to be touched. It probably would like it best just to crawl under some damp leaves in your garden.

Can a skunk smell the odor it makes?

Melanie Lyons
Tompkinsville, Kentucky

I don't know the answer and I am not sure just how to find out. Out in the wild skunks do not always smell bad. They smell only because of a special fluid which they can squirt out of their back end. Unless it has a reason to be afraid, a skunk does not squirt. It just raises its tail and stamps its feet. For most animals that is enough of a warning.

It has been observed that when one skunk fights with another, neither of them do any squirting. So some people think that the special fluid does not smell so good to a skunk, either. But I do not know how to be sure that this is right.

Can porcupines shoot quills at each other?

Jack Busboom
Langley Air Force Base, Virginia

I do not believe that porcupines need to protect themselves from another porcupine very often. I have never seen two porcupines fighting, nor have I read that such fights occur.

Porcupines may sometimes fight during the mating season, but I do not believe such fights are especially serious. If they do fight, I suspect they swing their tails back and forth as though they were fighting some other animal. The quills that cover most of the body would protect the animals from the quills of the other porcupine. But the animals do occasionally get quills in unprotected parts of the body such as the front legs.

When a porcupine gets quilled, it pulls the quill out. They have been seen to use their front legs to remove quills that are not very deep, and to use their teeth to dislodge quills that are stuck in more deeply.

Porcupines do not pick fights with other animals. They seem to be satisfied to go waddling and grunting along, eating bark and other plant parts, and not paying any attention to what other animals are doing. They do not appear to be afraid of other animals, but act as though they are well protected. And of course the quills do give them very good protection.

Porcupines are sometimes attacked by other animals that are trying to collect a nice fat porcupine to eat. A porcupine that is attacked will erect its quills, then back toward the other animal swinging its tail back and forth. If the animal attacking is foolish enough to be hit by the tail, it often gets a face full of quills for its trouble.

O.P.B.

Every dog I know goes around and around in circles before lying down. Could you tell me why they do this?

Rhonda Willoughby
High River, Alberta

I have heard the idea that the circling before lying down is a behavior inherited from wild ancestors. Maybe it was a way of making a nest in tall weeds or grass.

That sounds reasonable though I cannot be sure it is the best explanation. If you find a better explanation, please let me know.

Is it true that cats, dogs, and maybe other animals can hear things that people can't?

Alisha Olmsted
Lake Ann, Michigan

Dogs can hear sounds of higher frequency, or higher pitch, than your ear can hear. You can buy dog whistles that make high-pitched sounds just for calling a dog. Recent studies on elephants show that they seem to communicate through sounds that have a pitch so low—even lower than that of a big drum—that people can't hear it.

So, I guess the answer to your question is yes.

My dog sometimes eats our grass and then throws up. Why does she eat the grass if she will throw up?

Dana Kern
Los Gatos, California

That seems a rather common thing for dogs to do. We had a dog that used to do that. I think our dog felt sick before she ate grass. Dogs throw up rather easily, much more readily than people do. It occurs to me that maybe eating grass is a way a dog uses to help it throw up.

You can see that I really do not know the answer. If I were you I would ask your veterinarian, who probably will have a simple answer.

Do dogs have good eyesight? My dog sometimes barks at our garbage cans.

Timmy Green
Chicago, Illinois

I always supposed that dogs have good eyesight. However, maybe some of them have problems with their eyes just as humans do.

I also should tell you that I have seen dogs bark at very strange things for no reason that I could understand.

Maybe you can invent some way to test your dog's eyesight. Will it run to get a stick or ball that you throw? If it can do that its eyesight must be OK. Or maybe you can think of some other trick.

43

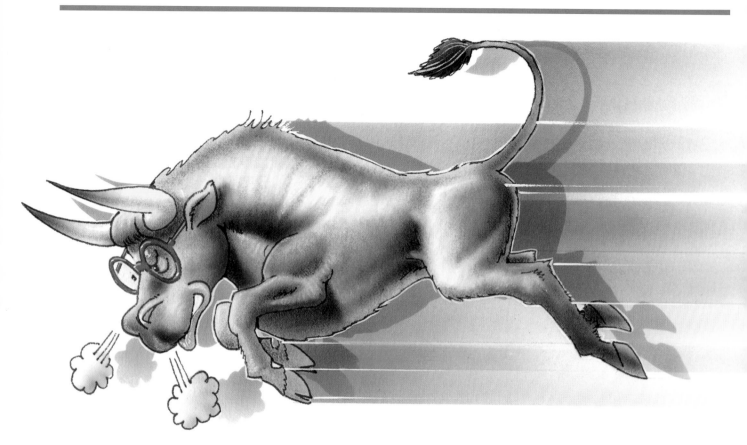

Can bulls really see red?

Sarah Arbuckle
New Boston, Missouri

I thought I knew the answer because other readers had asked me that question. The standard answer has been that, of all the mammals, only humans and apes have color vision. If that is true, then we would have to say that bulls do not see red because they are color-blind. But this idea comes from a book that was published in 1942. When I went to the library to check again, I found that there have been a lot more studies on color vision in animals since then.

Finding out about color vision in people is easy because people can tell us what they see. But how do you find out in animals?

One way is to teach the animal to play a game to see whether it can tell if two spots of light are the same or different. Can the animal tell that a yellow spot and an orange spot are different? Can it tell a yellow spot from spots with shades of gray? Not all studies have agreed.

I found one study on color vision in cows done by scientists in Poland. They found that their cows could see the differences between seven different colors ranging from blue to red. They believed, but did not prove, that a red color made cows more excitable.

I think we can suppose that bulls are like cows in their color vision. It seems that bulls can see red all right. And it might even turn out that the red color chosen for a bullfighter's cape may be the best color to excite a bull.

I also learned about a recent, very careful study of color vision in dogs. Dogs easily see differences between blues and greens and yellows. But they are not very good at seeing differences between yellows and oranges and reds. So it seems that dogs see colors about the same as some people who are said to be red-green color-blind.

I suspect that the question of whether an animal has color vision will someday be answered, not by yes or no, but by how much.

I've always wanted to know if animals such as dogs and cats have languages of their own. Do they?

Shannon Williams
Bethesda, Maryland

If you have a dog of your own or have watched two dogs playing together, you already know part of the answer. A dog has a way of telling things to other dogs, maybe just by the way it barks or growls or maybe just by the way it holds its tail.

Different kinds of animals have different ways of telling things to each other. In fact, whole books are written about animal communication. In general, it seems the social animals—the kinds that live together in groups—develop better ways of talking to each other. Most cats are loners and less social than dogs. But even a cat has a way of telling another cat it doesn't like him—at least if it wants to.

Of course, there is also another part to the answer. The things that animals can say to each other are really pretty simple. No animal could say, "I can't come out until five o'clock because I have to take care of my baby sister and then do my homework." But you might say that. You can put sounds together to make words. You can put words together to make ideas. And you do all that so well that another person knows exactly what you are thinking.

Maybe that's what you mean by "language." If you do, then you have to say that other animals do not have a real language, only ways of giving some signals for simple ideas.

I guess the answer to your question depends on what you think language really is.

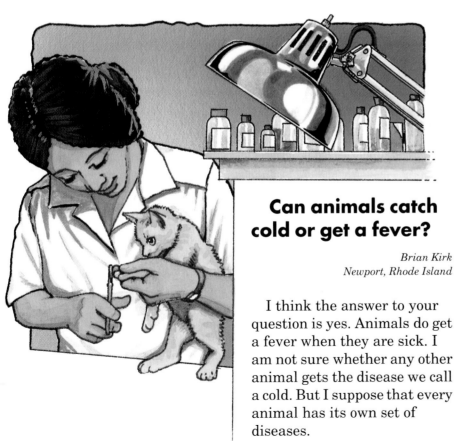

Can animals catch cold or get a fever?

Brian Kirk
Newport, Rhode Island

I think the answer to your question is yes. Animals do get a fever when they are sick. I am not sure whether any other animal gets the disease we call a cold. But I suppose that every animal has its own set of diseases.

There are some diseases of animals which humans can get, too. One of these is rabies, which occurs in dogs and wild animals such as foxes, bats, and squirrels. A person bitten by a sick animal can get the rabies virus which causes the disease. Dogs usually are vaccinated to protect them from rabies.

There is one way in which diseases are less of a problem for wild animals than for people. People often live close together. And often we spend some time rather close to other people, as in buses, classrooms, and theaters. That makes it easier for diseases to be transferred from one person to another. Wild animals seldom crowd together the way we do and their diseases do not spread so easily.

Did unicorns really exist?

Tammy Tovar
San Francisco, California

I am sorry to tell you that the answer is no. The unicorn is an imaginary animal, maybe based on the stories of someone who had seen a rhinoceros. A lot of people must have liked that idea because there seem to be lots of pictures of unicorns. But no one has found any bones or fossil of an animal that could have looked like the pictures.

Why do tigers like to swim when other members of the cat family do not?

Levi Klau
Ashville, New York

I have read that tigers not only swim but even like to bathe. However, I have never seen a tiger do that.

I don't know how to answer the "why" part and I am not sure that anyone can. Most tigers live in Southeast Asia where there are lots of streams and rivers. Maybe they learned to swim just because there is so much water where they live. Lions and mountain lions live in drier country and might not have to cross streams. Do you think this is a sensible idea?

Why do certain animals live in specific places?

Shaylee Nevez
Portola, California

Each kind of animal lives in a particular kind of place, which you can call its habitat. There is a basic reason for that. In nature, animals are always in competition. They struggle to survive.

You will notice that the animals in any particular habitat seem well suited or adapted to live there. A sea lion's front and back legs have become flippers and are good for swimming. Sea lions are great at living in the ocean and catching fish to eat. You can easily see that a buffalo could never live in the sea lion's habitat. But it's also easy to see that a sea lion could never live on the grassland of the buffalo's habitat.

I guess we could say that to compete in its habitat, an animal must become a specialist. But being a specialist helps in only one habitat and is likely to be a problem in others.

Plants are also limited to particular habitats. The cactus is good at living in the desert, a water lily can live only in water, and a pine tree is good at living on snowy mountainsides.

Why is bird watching popular?

Vivek Vinair
Falls Church, Virginia

I have friends who are bird watchers. But I don't know any who say they are reptile watchers or mammal watchers or fish watchers. I guess that's why you asked the question.

Bird watching is something anyone can do. Birds move around so much that anyone can get to see them. And we can bring them in closer with feeders or birdhouses. Watching them doesn't cost much and is easy to do.

An enthusiastic bird watcher could probably give you more reasons, but perhaps you can think of some others yourself.

Do cats have souls?

Briana Bathrick
Wales, Massachusetts

That's a very heavy question and one that I am not really qualified to answer. My own idea is that you have something deep inside that is the spiritual part of you. But after I have said that I don't know what to say next.

But you asked about cats. I don't know about that or even how to find out. I did wonder why you asked the question.

Maybe you had a cat that died and you miss it very much.

Until a few years ago I had a cat, Jackie, that had lived with us for a long time. She was a people-loving cat. When my wife and I played badminton in the afternoon, she would stretch out on a bench just to watch us. I still remember all the little things she did that made us love her. Now that she is gone I sometimes catch myself looking to see if she is stretched out on that bench again.

Maybe that great memory I have could be called a part of Jackie's soul. I guess that's the best I can do in answering your question.

Could a bird on its way to the Arctic possibly get lost where I live in Bear, Delaware?

Jana O'Grady
Bear, Delaware

I just have to say I don't know. You must have seen some strange and unusual bird. I think you might look in the Peterson bird guide. It shows migration routes for different birds. Maybe you are on a flyway path for some birds.

I have wondered what could happen to one of the birds in a long nonstop flight. What would happen if one got tired? Maybe it would just stop to rest awhile. What do you think?

North Pole ~ 2700 mi.

LA~2500

Miami 1000

49

Why are bugs attracted to light? I turned on the light outside our house, and all the bugs flew around it.

Heidi Greger
Rockford, Michigan

I am sorry that I cannot tell you why bugs are attracted to light. But I can tell you a few other things about insects and light. Some bugs or insects are attracted to light, but others go away from light. We say that those that move away from light are repelled. Cockroaches are insects that are repelled by light. They usually hide in dark places such as under the sink, behind drawers, and in cracks.

Certain kinds of light attract insects more than others. White light and blue light attract them more than do red or yellow light. Some people use yellow bulbs outside their houses. Insects do not fly around yellow bulbs as much as they do around white bulbs.

Sometimes young insects are not attracted to lights, but grown insects of the same kind are attracted. For example, cricket eggs hatch in the spring. The young crickets grow in the spring and early summer. You do not see many young crickets around lights. When the crickets get grown in the late summer and fall, they sometimes get together in large groups. In some cities in the United States these grown crickets are attracted to lights in the late summer and fall.

If large numbers of crickets are attracted to lights, they can cause trouble. They fly and hop around the lights and get on people when they pass, and people do not like to be covered by flying, hopping crickets!

I would like to know if an insect has ears. This question has been bugging me for a long time.

Meg Wallace
Middletown, Pennsylvania

Many insects do indeed have ears, although they do not look very much like ours. And the ears of many insects are not on their heads. They are on parts of the body that seem strange to us.

The ears of grasshoppers, crickets, and katydids are rather easy to find. Those of grasshoppers are at the base of the tail, one on each side, near the last pair of legs. Each ear looks like a small, shiny piece of cellophane.

The ears are really small membranes that work something like our eardrums.

The ears of crickets and katydids are on the front legs. Each is in a very small depression on the upper part of the leg joint just above the foot. These ears also have small shiny membranes, but they are so small that the membranes are hard to see. The ears of certain other insects are on other parts of the body.

The "feelers" or antennas on the heads of mosquitoes are used for their ears. When a mosquito flies, the wings move so fast that they make a humming or singing sound. We call this sound the song of the mosquito.

The male (or papa) mosquito can "hear" or receive the female mosquito's song with his antennas. The song tells a male mosquito that nearby there is a female mosquito that is the same kind of mosquito that he is. The male mosquito can follow the song.

Why do animals have four legs?

Stacy Mackingu
Torrance, California

I guess you are thinking about the larger animals. The amphibians (like frogs), reptiles (like lizards), birds, and mammals are all called tetrapods, which means four-footed. Of course the birds have two wings instead of two legs. And humans have two arms in place of two legs. And there are some special kinds like snakes which seem to have lost their legs.

But why is four legs the general plan? I don't know.

You should also consider that the most successful group of animals is the insects. They have more different kinds (probably more than a million species), and they live in more different kinds of places than any other group. They have six legs. So maybe four is not so wonderful.

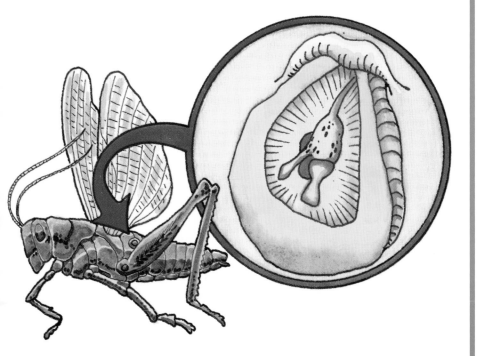

Why does a snake's tongue flash out?

Ronald Durbin
Rochester, New York

Almost everyone knows that as a snake crawls along, its tongue flicks in and out of its mouth. Most people also know that the tongue is forked. Both the flicking habit and the fact that the tongue is forked are unusual among animals. Because these things are unusual, some people believe that snakes bite with their tongues.

Snakes of course do not bite with their tongues, but it is quite useful to the snake to flick the tongue in and out of its mouth. The tongue is a very important sense organ. The snake, of course, has no fingers or toes with which to feel. The tongue has a sense of touch, and because of this, the tongue somewhat takes the place of fingers and toes. The snake can smell with its nose, but the tongue helps the nose because it also has a sense of smell.

The sense of touch and the sense of smell in the tongue help the snake to find its food. The tongue also helps the snake to find another snake during the mating season.

O.P.B.

In pond water there are tiny animals such as protozoans. When the water evaporates, do these tiny animals evaporate, too?

Denise Vitola
West Atlantic City, New Jersey

When a pond dries up, most of the little animals dry up and die. A few of them are covered up in the mud and leaves at the bottom and, if the pond does not get too dry, they can go on living. Some of them form cysts, which are little round bodies with tough walls which are very resistant. When they get wet again the cysts change back into normal cells that swim away.

All micro-organisms, including the protozoa, can be carried by wind or on blowing leaves or on the feet of water birds. So a dried-up pond, or even a brand-new pond, suddenly filled with water soon gets micro-organisms from outside. And micro-organisms can multiply so fast that a few starters can soon grow into thousands more.

As you can see, the life of any one individual among the littlest animals is rather precarious. Usually there are so many that we do not pay much attention to what happens to any one of them.

I heard that camels store fat, not water, in their humps. So how does fat help them survive in the desert?

Chani Lefkowitz
Brooklyn, New York

Camels do store some fat in their humps, but that is not an explanation of their survival in the desert. They let their body temperature slowly increase during a hot day and then cool back down at night. They don't sweat so much during the day, partly protected from the sun by tight hairs on their backs.

Camels don't have any one special secret. Their bodies just do several things a little differently.

What is the smallest animal?

Steve Taylor
Menomonee Falls, Wisconsin

Deciding on just what is the smallest animal is not so easy. I suppose it must be one of the many one-celled protozoans that can be seen under a microscope.

However, you may really be thinking: What's the smallest mammal? I think the answer to that is a shrew. Shrews are tiny mouselike animals that are so sneaky that they are seldom seen.

One book I have says that the smallest is the pygmy shrew. It is only about one-and-one-half inches long and could hide in a tablespoon. I wonder how big its babies are?

Do animals cry the way people do?

Ashley Katen
Glenrock, Wyoming

Cats and dogs and most other animals have lacrimal glands. These glands produce tears, which moisten the front of the eye and help keep it clean. If some dirt gets in the eyes, the glands make extra tears that spill over and run down outside. I guess you could call that crying.

But you probably are thinking of crying as something people do when they are hurt or very sad. I have never seen any other animal do that.

The lacrimal glands are controlled by nerve messages from the brain. In your brain, you must also have some special nerve pathways that allow emotions to affect the glands. As far as I can find out, other animals do not have those pathways.

If you can find more information about this, please let me know.

I have always wanted to know what the biggest dinosaur was. Some of my books say it was Brontosaurus, some Brachiosaurus, others Ultrasaurus, some Seismosaurus, and one says it was Breviparopus.

Nicholas Goffee
New Concord, Ohio

I didn't know the answer so I asked my friend, Wann Langston, who has spent his life studying dinosaurs. Here is what he said:

There are a number of candidates that seem to be bigger than Brontosaurus. One is Ultrasaurus, another (maybe bigger) is Supersaurus, and still another (maybe bigger yet) is Seismosaurus.

Here's the problem. No one has found a complete skeleton of any of these very large, plant-eating dinosaurs. Instead we may have a legbone from one, a shoulder from another, maybe some of the backbones of another. It's easy to tell that they had to be very big animals. It's hard to tell which was the biggest.

How come dinosaurs had such small brains? To control their bodies would seem to need a larger brain.

Greg Lanier
San Jose, California

I can see why you might wonder why animals as large as dinosaurs should have small brains.

Of course, no one has seen a dinosaur brain. We know that they must have been small because of the small size of their skulls.

The dinosaur you probably are thinking about was Brontosaurus, the Thunder Lizard. From fossil bones it has been estimated that this critter weighed as much as thirty-five tons but had a brain which could hardly have weighed as much as a pound. Sometimes it is said that Brontosaurus also had a second brain at the base of its tail. Actually this so-called second brain must have been just an enlarged part of its spinal cord.

In the nervous system the job of controlling muscles and body parts is done mostly in the spinal cord. So just managing a big body does not necessarily require a big brain. The brain is the part of the nervous system which does the job we call thinking.

I suspect that Brontosaurus did not do much thinking. In fact, some people have suggested that that is one reason why Brontosaurus and the other dinosaurs perished from the earth. I guess the idea is that smarter animals came along.

How do lungless animals breathe? I am thinking particularly about insects like ants.

Jonathan Kibler
Claremont, California

Insects like the ant have a simple breathing system made of small tubes called trachea that extend from the body surface to someplace inside. Insects don't breathe the way you do, but movements of their muscles squeeze the trachea and push a little air in and out.

I know most animals have bones. But what about ants?

Tessa Butzke
Los Angeles, California

The answer is no, ants don't have bones. As other insects, an ant wears its skeleton on the outside, so it is called an exoskeleton. And it really isn't made of bone but of a stuff called chitin.

Since there are more kinds of insects than of any other group of animals, I guess we have to decide that most animals do not have bones. That may seem a surprise just because most of the big animals we see do have bones like ours.

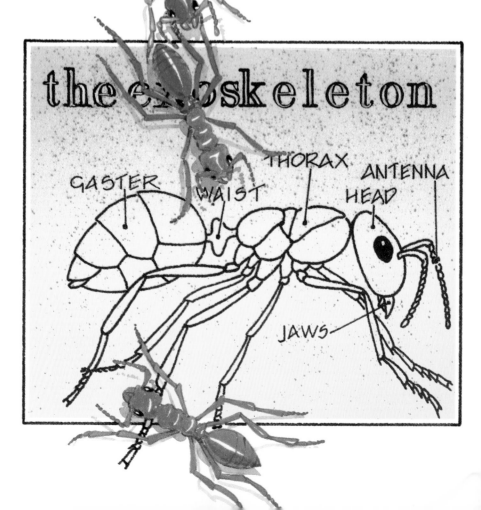

the exoskeleton

GASTER WAIST THORAX ANTENNA HEAD JAWS

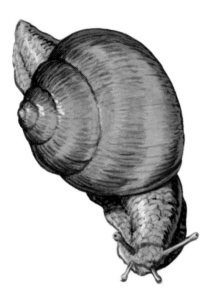

What do snails eat? And what happens when a snail does not have a shell? Does it grow a new one or find one?

Nejla Milanana
Williamsport, Maryland

There are many different kinds of snails. Most of them live on plant material. The ones that live in water usually move slowly over rocks, picking up algae as they go. Some people like to have snails in aquaria because they work like small vacuum cleaners to suck the green scum of algae off the glass.

The snails have close relatives, the slugs, which are like naked snails without any shells. The snails are their own house builders and each one makes its own shell. That seems like a lot of work. But if you watch a snail, you soon realize that it is never in a hurry and has lots of time.

Do ostriches still swallow pebbles after eating? I read about it in Swiss Family Robinson, so I was wondering.

Jodie Mangawang
Waco, Texas

I don't know when an ostrich is likely to swallow pebbles, but I would expect it to do so rather often. Like other birds, it really doesn't chew its food the way we do. Instead it has a gizzard, a pouch with heavy muscle walls, which grinds up its food.

Most birds have some grit or fine stones in the gizzard to help. So I suppose a bird as big as an ostrich would be using pebbles.

Why do a dog's legs thump when you scratch its back or tummy?

Sara Stallard
Campbell, California

I have noticed that, too. If you try that some more on your dog, you will find that you have to scratch at a special place. Scratching behind a dog's ears won't work.

I think that you are talking about what is called the "scratch reflex." This is one of those automatic actions of an animal's body. These reflexes depend on muscles and nerves but do not depend upon thinking in the brain.

The scratch reflex is complicated because it makes a lot of leg muscles work just by lightly scratching special places, usually on a dog's side. I think it is supposed to work on other animals, too.

Why aren't cats fierce and dangerous like lions, tigers, and mountain lions?

Patricia Hays
Frankston, Texas

You are right about that. Our common house cats are safe to live with. Of course, they have been living with people for several thousand years. They have become different from wild cats in much the same way that dogs are different from wolves.

You may notice that even house cats still have some wild streaks. I think we feed our cat pretty well. But she still goes out hunting for birds and mice. She sometimes makes a mess by bringing back a dead bird and scattering feathers all over our front porch.

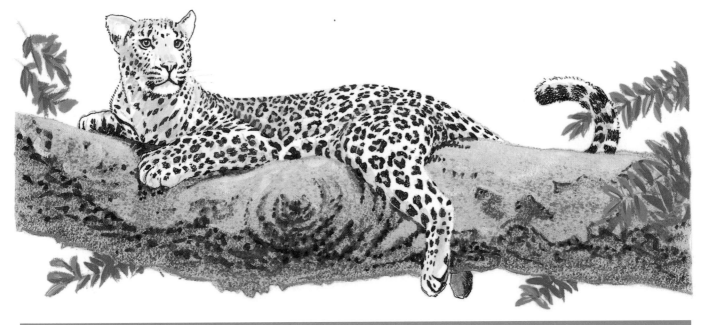

I know that the temperature of a dog is higher than a human's, but what is its exact normal temperature?

Laila Kafrawy
Flemington, New Jersey

I did not know the answer and had to look it up in a book on domestic animals. For a dog the average rectal temperature is given at 102 degrees Fahrenheit, and the normal temperature range is given as 100.2 to 103.8 degrees F. The normal rectal temperature of a human is supposed to be 98.6 degrees F.

You are right that dogs run a little warmer than humans. However, there is no exact "normal" temperature. Body temperature is not exactly the same in all individuals. And your temperature may vary about one degree during the course of a day. Probably a dog's temperature will, too.

When I looked this up I was surprised at the number of animals that have had their temperatures taken. One that caught my eye was the skunk, body temperature 97.5 degrees F. It must have taken a very curious person to find that out!

59

Where do fish go in the winter for shelter?

Mary Houghton
Albany, New York

I think you asked that question because in New York State, where you live, most streams and lakes are covered with ice in the winter. However, very few lakes and large streams freeze all the way to the bottom. Ice provides pretty good insulation against heat flow. And since the ice always floats as a layer on top, the water underneath is protected and doesn't freeze.

You also might think about how neat it is that ice does float. If it did not, then lakes would freeze from the bottom up, and that would be bad for the fish.

How do fish breathe?

Lora Toney
Gastonia, North Carolina

You and I usually think about breathing as the moving of air into and out of our lungs. The important event occurs in our lungs. That is where we take up oxygen and get rid of carbon dioxide.

Some water animals, such as turtles and whales, do their breathing about the same way we do. But fish and other water animals do their breathing (if we can call it that) right from the water itself. Instead of lungs, they have gills.

In most fishes the gills are just behind the mouth, one on each side. Most fishes, when they are not swimming, slowly move their gill flaps to pump water through them. If you look closely at the gills of a fish, you will see that inside they have thin, flimsy rows of red tissue. They are red because of the many blood vessels close to the surface of the tissue. That is where a fish gets its oxygen from the water.

I have four fishes in a plastic aquarium. I have noticed that the water starts to go green about four days after I clean it. Would you please explain why the aquarium goes green?

Susanna Morey
Nagano Ken, Japan

I think your aquarium gets green because of algae that grow in its water. There are many different kinds of these which are microscopic in size and made out of single cells, the tiniest of plants. When there are enough of them in an aquarium, they will make the water look greenish.

In aquariums and swimming pools, algae are considered a nuisance. In ponds and rivers and oceans algae are important because they are the plants which support all the animals that live in the water.

Sometimes algae are called the "grasses of the ocean" or the beginning of the "food chain." Here is the idea. The tiny algae are food for tiny animals; the tiny animals are food for little fish; and little fish are food for bigger fish. The best fishing places in the ocean are those which also have the most algae.

I suppose you would like to keep algae from growing in your aquarium and making the water green. Of course, there are chemicals which kill algae but most of these are not good for our fish. Algae need light and you could keep them from growing by keeping your aquarium in the dark—but that would not be much fun. However, you might try keeping your aquarium someplace which does not get too much light. And when you clean your aquarium, you should clean it carefully to get rid of all the algae you can.

You might be interested to know that I purposely grow algae in my laboratory. I have spent most of my life studying photosynthesis, the process that all plants use to make their own food using light energy. Photosynthesis in algae works just about the same as it does in the leaf of a tree. And in some ways algae are easier to manage.

I could say a lot more about algae, but maybe I already have told you more than you wanted to know.

How does an animal get its name?

Howard Cheung
Vancouver, British Columbia

Scientists who keep track of animals (and plants) have very strict rules for scientific names. The scientist who first describes an animal has the privilege of giving it a scientific name. As you may know, the scientific name is in Latin and always in two words. *Ursus horribilis* is the grizzly bear and *Ursus Americanus* is the black bear. They both belong to the genus Ursus, but each has its own species name.

Common names are likely to be different in different languages. I doubt that it is known just who invented the common names.

In school I read that reptiles lay eggs. I've been wondering if birds are reptiles or mammals.

Dawn McKnight
Gibraltar, Michigan

Birds do not fit in either classification. The animal kingdom is broken down into invertebrates (animals without backbones) and vertebrates (animals with backbones). There are several classes under the heading vertebrate including bony fishes, amphibians, reptiles, mammals, and birds.

Birds are special enough that scientists have decided to put them in a class of their own.

Are there any animals on earth that man does not know about?

Jim Gardner
Capac, Michigan

If you mean large land animals, like wolves or giraffes or elephants, then I doubt that there are any that some person has not seen. We humans are so curious that we have rather carefully explored the surface of our earth. One place we have not explored very well is the depths of the oceans.

It was a big surprise about fifty years ago when a previously unknown fish was caught off the coast of South Africa. And it was not just a little fish. It was about five feet long and weighed 127 pounds. It belonged to an interesting group of fishes called the Coelacanths. Similar fish had been known only from fossil remains which were at least sixty million years old. So this discovery was quite a surprise.

I expect that we will find new and interesting fish and other marine animals as we keep exploring the oceans.

Even on the earth's surface there are many new kinds or species of small animals reported every year. This is especially true for the insects. No one has counted carefully all the known species of insects, but a common estimate is about 800,000. Some zoologists guess that actually there may be more than one million. If that guess is right, then it means that there are a lot of insects which we do not know about—at least scientifically.

Index